You're a
Special Blessing

If I had a single flower for every time
I think about you, I could walk
forever in my garden.

CLAUDIA A. GRANDÍ

May you grow to be as beautiful
as God meant you to be when
He first thought of you.

It is God's knowledge of me...His
constant presence in the garden of my
little life that guarantees my joy.

W. PHILLIP KELLER

Be glad for all God is planning for you.
Be patient...and prayerful always.

ROMANS 12:12 TLB

Into all our lives, in many simple,
familiar, homely ways, God infuses this
element of joy from the surprises of life,
which unexpectedly brighten our days
and fill our eyes with light.

ℚ

LONGFELLOW

The happiness of life is made up of little
things: a smile, a hug, a moment of
shared laughter.

ℚ

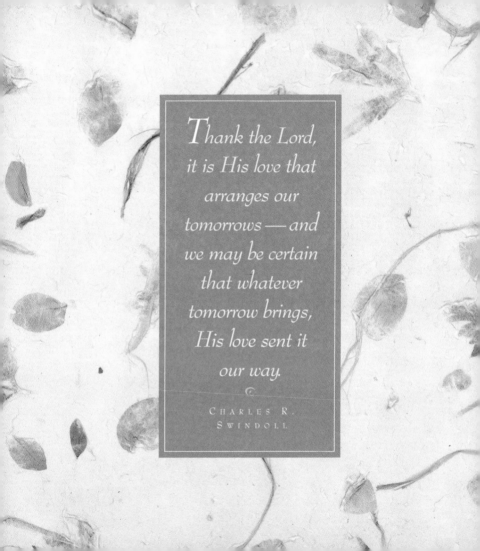

Thank the Lord, it is His love that arranges our tomorrows — and we may be certain that whatever tomorrow brings, His love sent it our way.

CHARLES R. SWINDOLL

*May you always find
three welcomes in life,
In a garden
during summer,
At a fireside during winter,
And whatever season
In the kind eyes of a friend.*

The best things are nearest: breath in
your nostrils, light in your eyes, flowers at
your feet, duties at your hand, the path
of God just before you.

ROBERT LOUIS STEVENSON

Happiness is the whole world as friends.
It's light all through your life.

DANIEL DILLING, AGE 8

Every moment is full of wonder,
and God is always present.

Lovely, complicated wrappings
Sheath the gift of one-day-more;
Breathless, I untie the package —
Never lived this day before!

GLORIA GAITHER

If God gives such attention to the appearance of wildflowers — most of which are never even seen — don't you think he'll attend to you, take pride in you, do his best for you? What I'm trying to do here is to get you to relax, to not be so preoccupied with *getting*, so you can respond to God's *giving*....

Steep your life in God-reality, God-initiative, God-provisions. Don't worry about missing out. You'll find all your everyday human concerns will be met. Give your entire attention to what God is doing right now, and don't get worked up about what may or may not happen tomorrow. God will help you deal with whatever hard things come up when the time comes.

MATTHEW 6:29-34 MSG

Cherish your visions;

cherish your ideals;

cherish the music

that stirs in your heart,

the beauty that forms

in your mind, the loveliness that

drapes your purest thoughts,

for out of them will grow

all delightful conditions,

all heavenly environment.

JAMES ALLEN

My heart is content with just knowing
The treasures of life's little things;
The thrill of a child when it's snowing,
The trill of a bird in the spring.

My heart is content with just knowing
Fulfillment that true friendship brings;
It fills to the brim, overflowing
With pleasure in life's "little things."

JUNE MASTERS BACHER

Life is God's gift to you. The way you
live your life is your gift to God.
Make it a fantastic one.

LEO BUSCAGLIA

And God is able to make all grace
abound to you, so that in all things at all
times, having all that you need, you will
abound in every good work.

2 CORINTHIANS 9:8 NIV

"Life's Ripples"

A tiny pebble idly tossed
Into the placid stream,
With gentle splash it sinks from sight
And not again is seen.
But outward from that central spot
The circling ripples tend;
Who knows on what far distant shore
The spreading impulse ends?
And so it is with life itself;
A kind thing we say or do
May take a moment of our time
And then be lost to view.
But ever onward it will go
And never lost shall be
Until its widening mission done,
It joins infinity.

EDWIN ROWORTH

Hold fast your dreams!
Within your heart keep
one still, secret spot
where dreams may go
and, sheltered so, may
thrive and grow where
doubt and fear are not.
O keep a place apart
within your heart, for
little dreams to go!

LOUISE DRISCOLL

*You never know
when someone may
catch a dream
from you.*

HELEN LOWRIE
MARSHALL

Our God is so wonderfully good,

and lovely, and blessed

in every way that the mere fact

of belonging to Him is enough

for an untellable fullness of joy!

HANNAH WHITALL SMITH

He made you so you could

share in His creation, could love

and laugh and know Him.

TED GRIFFEN

The joy that you give to others is
the joy that comes back to you.

JOHN GREENLEAF WHITTIER

May happiness touch your life today
as warmly as you have touched the
lives of others.

You are special, and not because
I've said so, but because forever
and always you have been a part
of God's plan.

❧

May the Lord bless and protect
you; may the Lord's face radiate
with joy because of you; may he
be gracious to you, show you his
favor, and give you His peace.

❧

NUMBERS 6:24-26 TLB